Popular Piano
For All Piano Method

MW00699926

Table of Contents

Popular Piano Solos Level 5 is designed for use with the fifth book of most piano methods.

Concepts in *Popular Piano Solos Level 5*:

Range

Symbols

pp, *p*, *mp*, *mf*, *f*, *ff*, *sfz*, ♯, ♭, ♮, *rit.*, *a tempo*, *sim.*, *8va*, *loco*, *D.S. al Fine*, 𝄋, 𝄐

cresc. ———— ———— *dim.*

Rhythm

time signatures: 2/4 3/4 4/4 ¢

swing eighths

Scales

Major: C	G	F	D	B♭
Minor: a	e	d	b	g

Chords

M, m, aug., dim.   1st and 2nd inversions

ISBN 0-634-02095-1

HAL•LEONARD®
CORPORATION

7777 W. BLUEMOUND RD. P.O. BOX 13819 MILWAUKEE, WI 53213

Visit Hal Leonard Online at
www.halleonard.com

Star Trek – The Next Generation®

Theme from the Paramount Television Series
STAR TREK: THE NEXT GENERATION®

By Alexander Courage,
Gene Roddenberry and Jerry Goldsmith
Arranged by Phillip Keveren

Can You Feel The Love Tonight

from Walt Disney Pictures' THE LION KING

Music by Elton John
Lyrics by Tim Rice
Arranged by Fred Kern

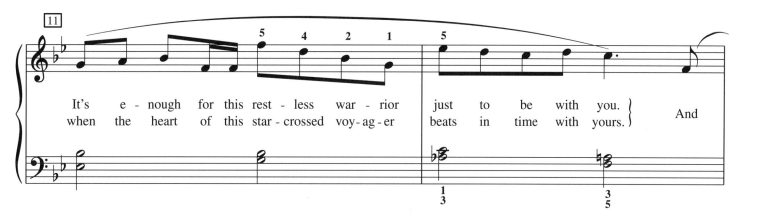

It's e - nough for this rest - less war - rior just to be with you.
when the heart of this star - crossed voy - ag - er beats in time with yours.

And

can you feel the love to - night? It is where we are.

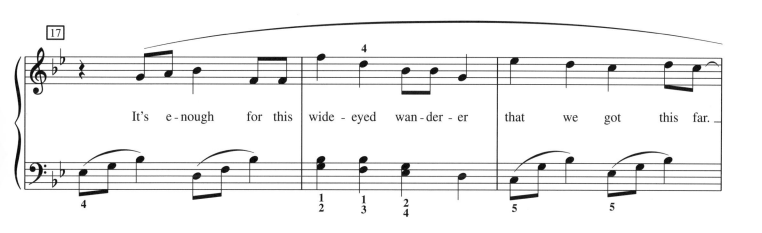

It's e - nough for this wide - eyed wan - der - er that we got this far.

And can you feel the love to - night,

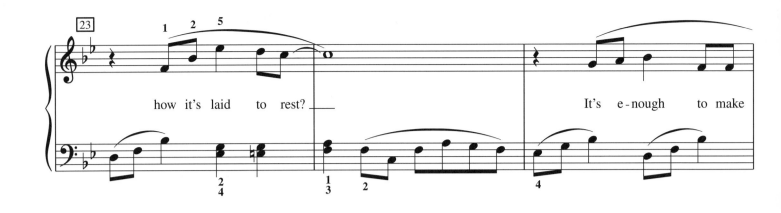

how it's laid to rest? _____ It's e-nough to make

kings and vag-a-bonds be - lieve the ver - y best.

Both hands 8va -

pp

2. Slower

It's e-nough to make kings and vag-a-bonds be - lieve the ver - y best.

mp

rit. e dim.

6

Ob-La-Di, Ob-La-Da

Words and Music by John Lennon
and Paul McCartney
Arranged by Carol Klose

life goes on   bra

la   la   how   their   life   goes   on.

And   if   you

want   some   fun   take

ob - la - di - bla - da.

Hey Jude

Words and Music by John Lennon
and Paul McCartney
Arranged by Carol Klose

Jude _____ don't be a - fraid.   You were made to _____ go out and
Jude _____ don't let me down.   You have found her, _____ now go and

get her. _____   The min - ute you let her un - der your
get her. _____   Re - mem - ber to let her in - to your

skin,   then you be - gin _____   to make it ____ bet - ter.
heart,   then you can start _____   to make it ____ bet - ter.

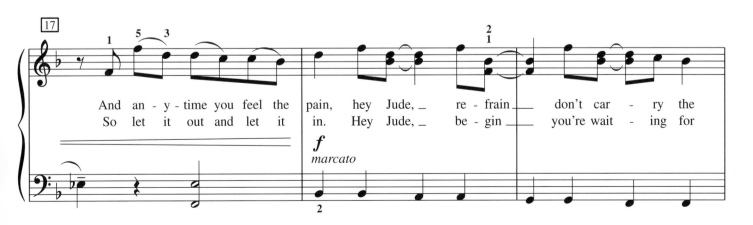

And an - y - time you feel the pain,   hey Jude, _ re - frain ____ don't car - ry the
So let it out and let it in.   Hey Jude, _ be - gin ____ you're wait - ing for

f
marcato

11

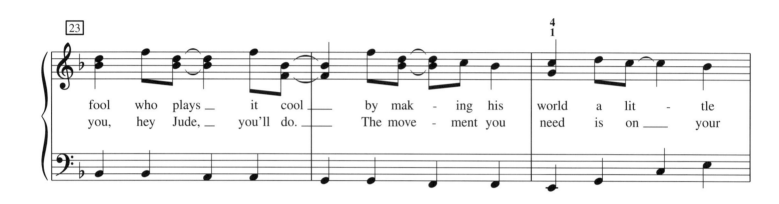

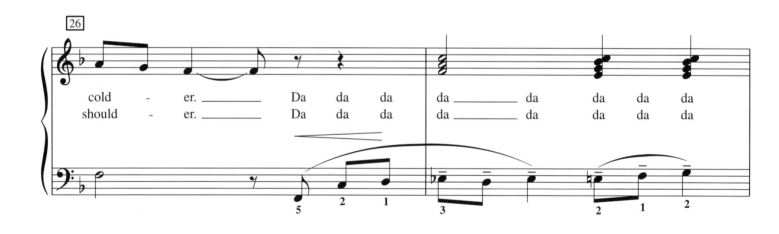

CODA

to make it bet — ter, bet - ter, bet - ter, bet - ter

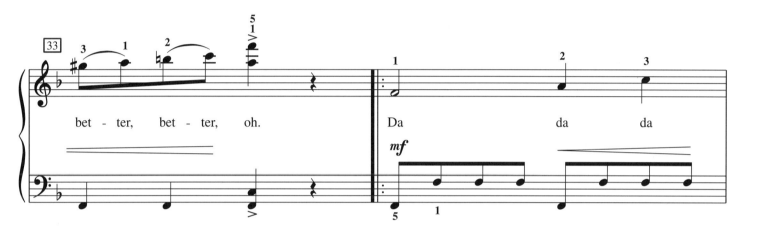

bet — ter, bet - ter, oh. Da da da

da da da da da da da da Hey ___

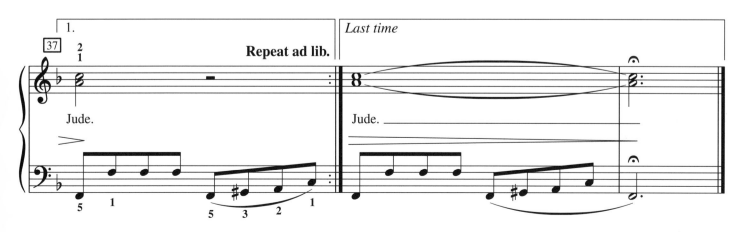

1.
Repeat ad lib.

Jude.

Last time

Jude. ___

13

Mission: Impossible Theme
from the Paramount Motion Picture MISSION: IMPOSSIBLE

By Lalo Schifrin
Arranged by Fred Kern

L.H. 8va - ┘ *loco*

L.H. 8va -

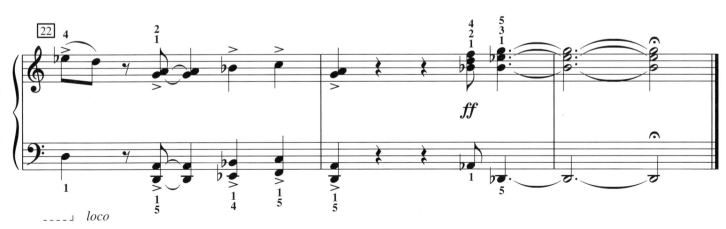

- - - - - ┘ *loco*

Chariots Of Fire
from CHARIOTS OF FIRE

By Vangelis
Arranged by Phillip Keveren

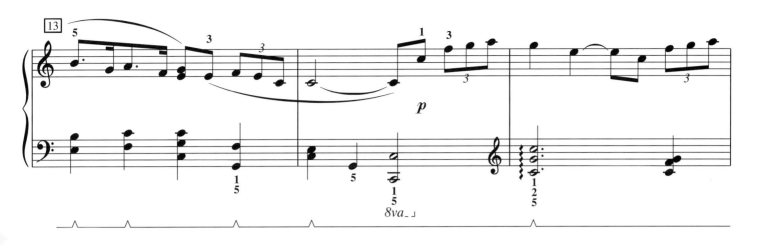

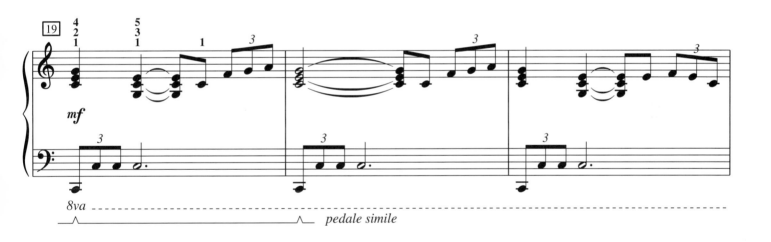

Y.M.C.A.

Words and Music by Jacques Morali,
Henri Belolo and Victor Willis
Arranged by Fred Kern

With a Disco beat

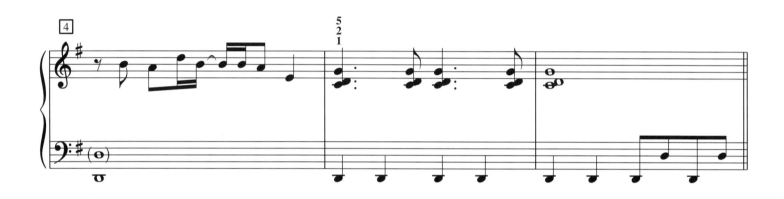

Young man, there's no need to feel down. _ I said, young man, pick your-

self off the ground. _ I said, young man, 'cause you're in a new town _ there's no

They have ev-er-y-thing _ for young men to en-joy. _ You can

hang out with all _ the boys. _ It's fun to stay at the Y. M. C. A.

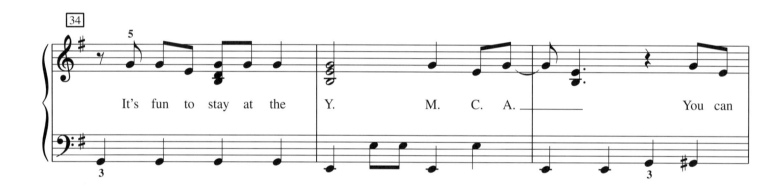

It's fun to stay at the Y. M. C. A. _ You can

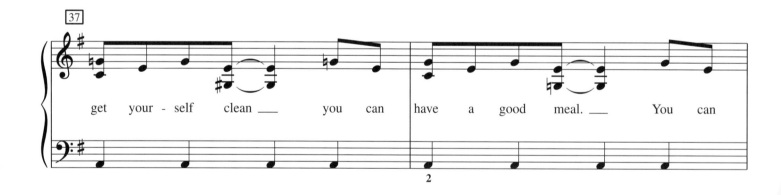

get your-self clean _ you can have a good meal. _ You can

do what-ev-er _ you feel. _

21

You've Got A Friend In Me

from Walt Disney's TOY STORY

Music and Lyrics by
Randy Newman
Arranged by Mona Rejino

Moderate Swing

you just re - mem - ber what your old pal said. Son,

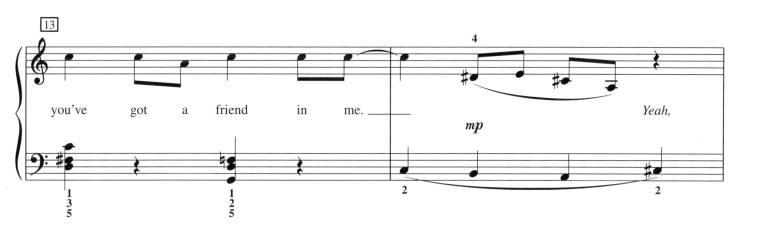

you've got a friend in me. *Yeah,*

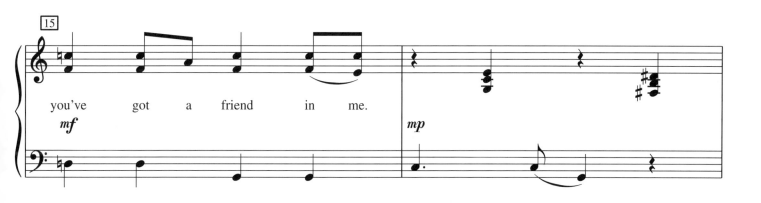

you've got a friend in me.

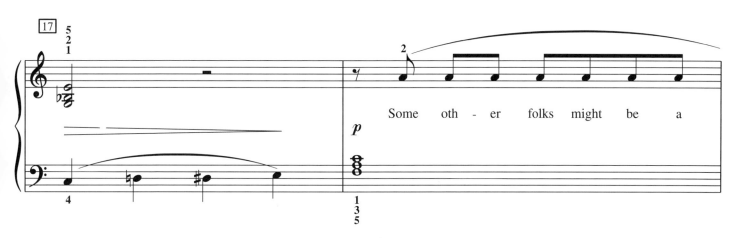

Some oth - er folks might be a

lit - tle bit smart - er than I am, big - ger and strong - er, too.

But none of them will ev - er love you ____ the
cresc. poco a poco

way I do, ____ just me and you, babe.

mf *f* And as the years go by, ____ our

friend - ship will nev - er die. ____ You're gon - na see it's our ____

Candle On The Water
from Walt Disney's PETE'S DRAGON

Words and Music by Al Kasha
and Joel Hirschhorn
Arranged by Phillip Keveren

Flowing

I'll be your can - dle on the
I'll be your can - dle on the

wa - ter,
wa - ter,

my love for you will al - ways
'til ev - 'ry wave is warm and

burn.
bright.

I know you're lost and drift - ing,
My soul is there be - side you,

but the clouds are lift - ing.
let this can - dle guide you.
Don't give up, you have some-where to turn.
Soon you'll see a gold - en stream of light.

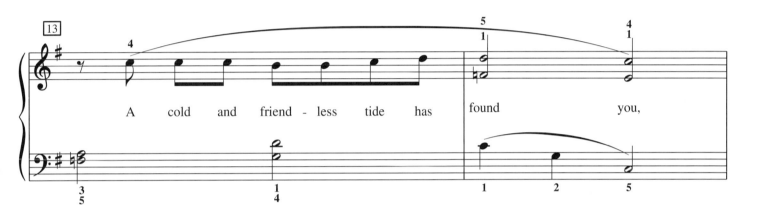

A cold and friend - less tide has found you,

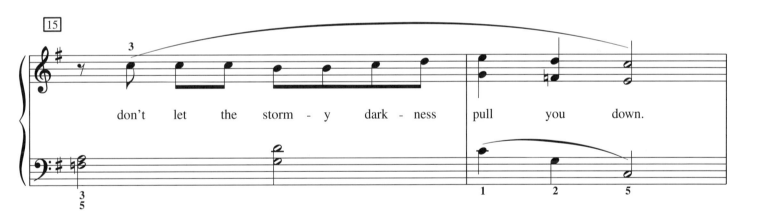

don't let the storm - y dark - ness pull you down.

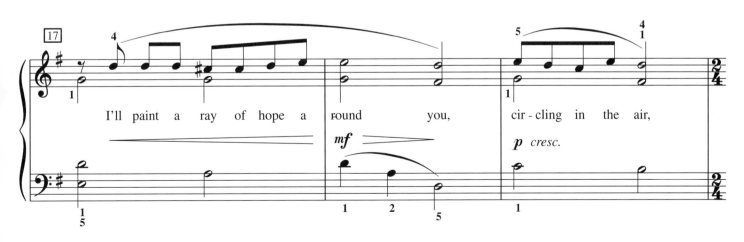

I'll paint a ray of hope a - round you, cir - cling in the air,

mf

p cresc.

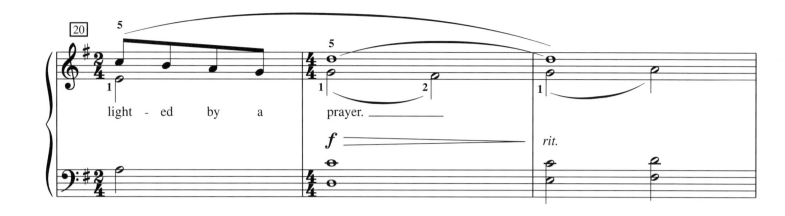

light - ed by a prayer. _____

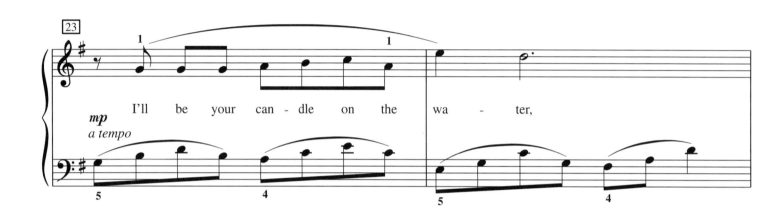

I'll be your can - dle on the wa - ter,

this flame in - side of me will grow. Keep hold - ing on, you'll make it.

Here's my hand so take it, look for me reach - ing out to

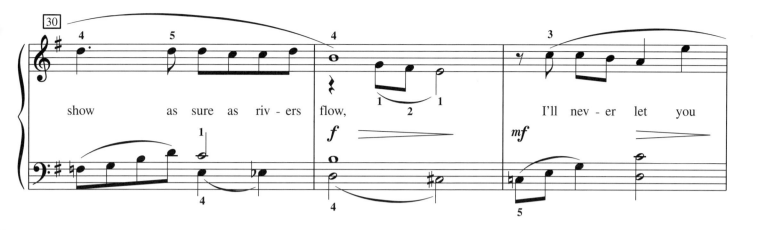

show   as sure as riv - ers flow,   I'll nev - er let you

go.   I'll nev - er let   you   go.

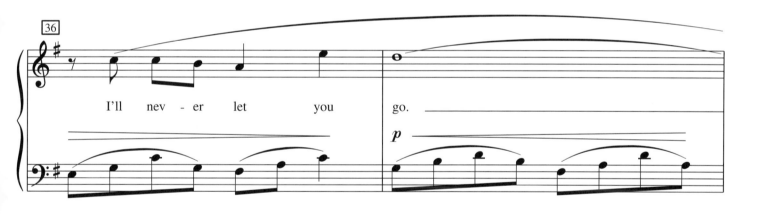

I'll nev - er let   you   go.

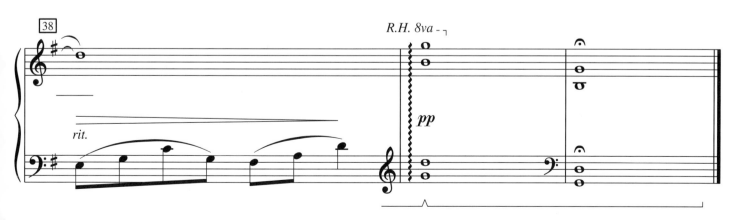

My Heart Will Go On
(Love Theme from 'Titanic')
from the Paramount and Twentieth Century Fox Motion Picture TITANIC

Music by James Horner
Lyric by Will Jennings
Arranged by Mona Rejino

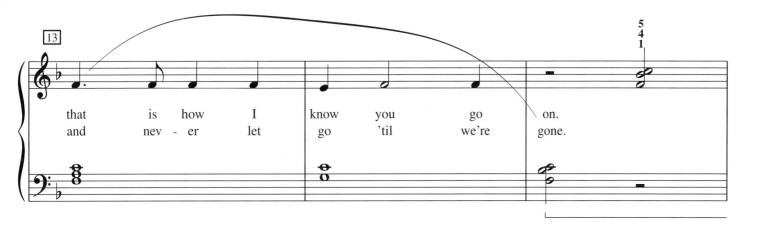

that is how I know you go on.
and nev - er let go you 'til we're on. gone.

Far a - cross the dis - tance and
Love was when I loved you; one

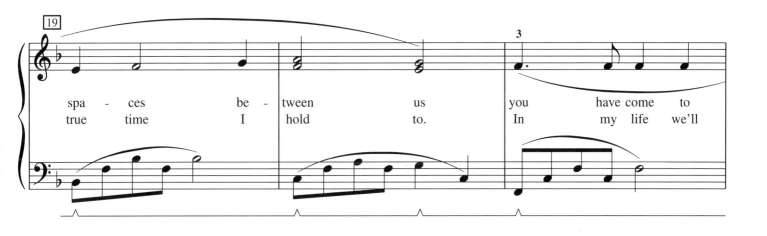

spa - ces be - tween us you have come to
true time I hold to. In my life we'll

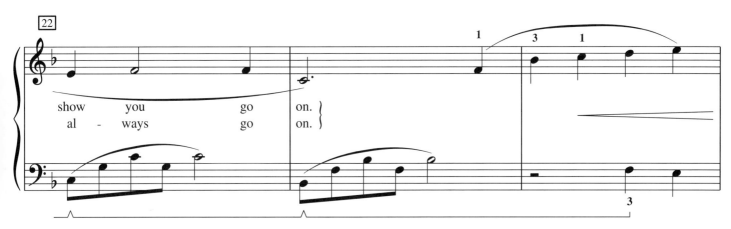

show you go on.
al - ways go on.

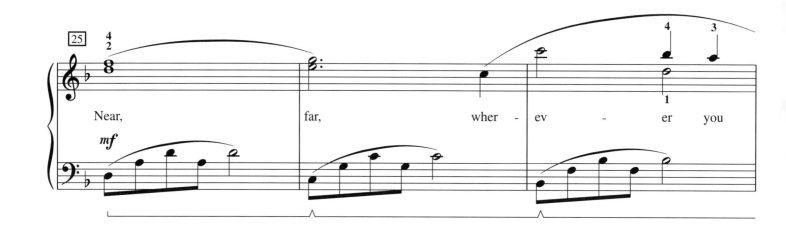

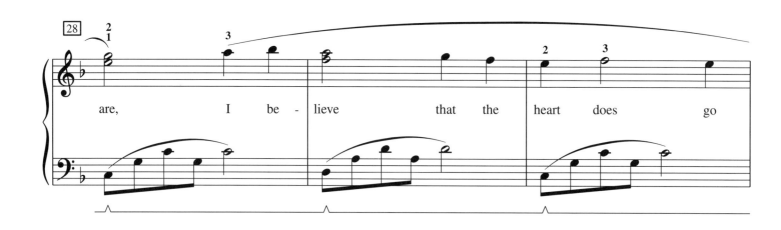

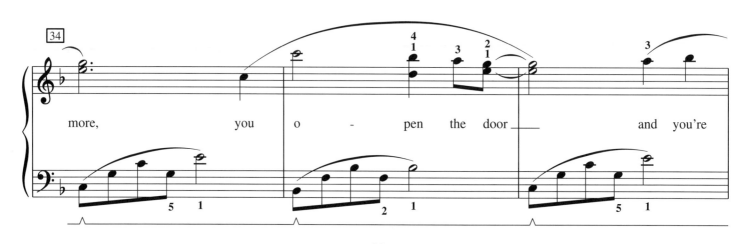

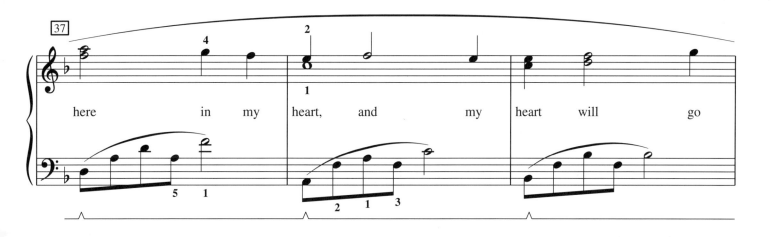

here   in   my   heart,   and   my   heart   will   go

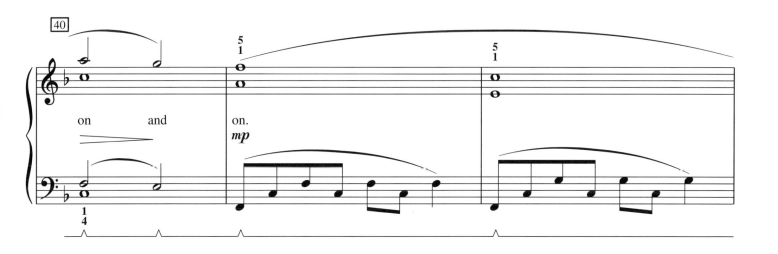

on   and   on. *mp*

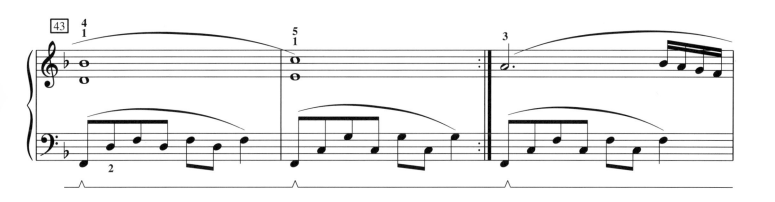

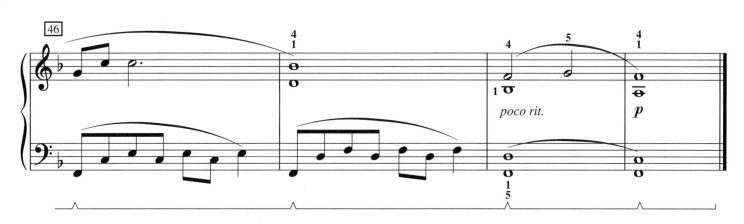

poco rit.   *p*

You'll Be In My Heart

from Walt Disney Pictures' TARZAN™

Words and Music by Phil Collins
Arranged by Mona Rejino

Lyrically

see in time, ____ I know, ____ we'll

show them to-geth-er. You'll be in my heart ____ no

mat-ter what they say. ____ You'll be here in my

heart al - ways.

I'll be there ____ al - ways.

36

Castle On A Cloud
from LES MISÉRABLES

Music by Claude-Michel Schönberg
Lyrics by Herbert Kretzmer
Original Text by Alain Boublil
and Jean-Marc Natel
Arranged by Carol Klose

Slowly, with expression

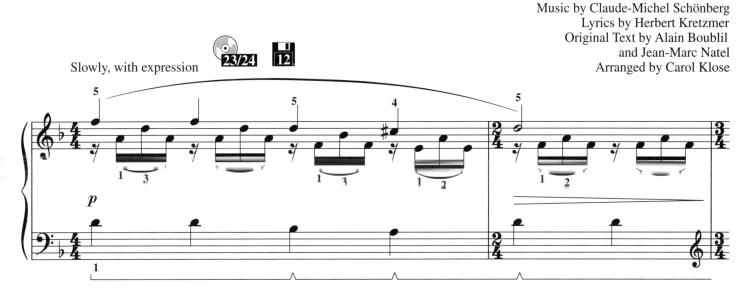

There is a cas - tle on a cloud.

I like to go there in my sleep.

Aren't an - y floors for me to sweep,

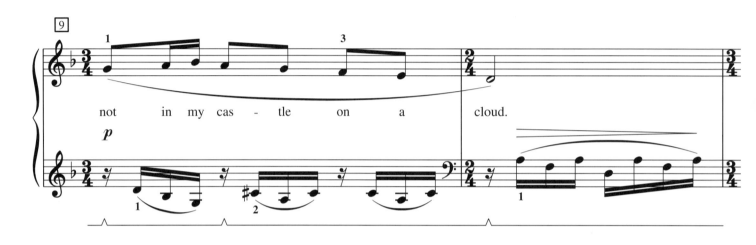

not in my cas - tle on a cloud.

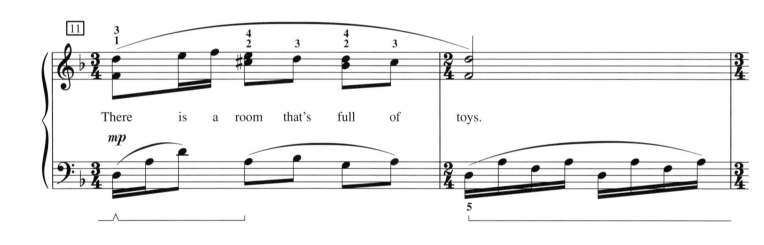

There is a room that's full of toys.

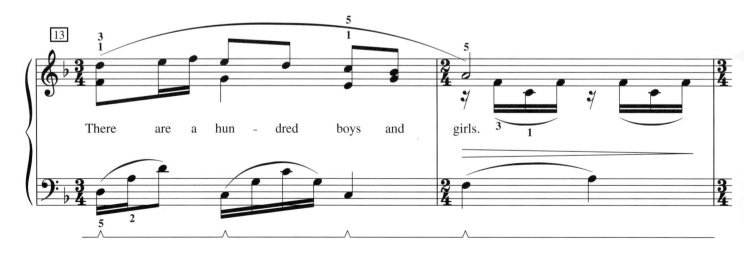

There are a hun - dred boys and girls.

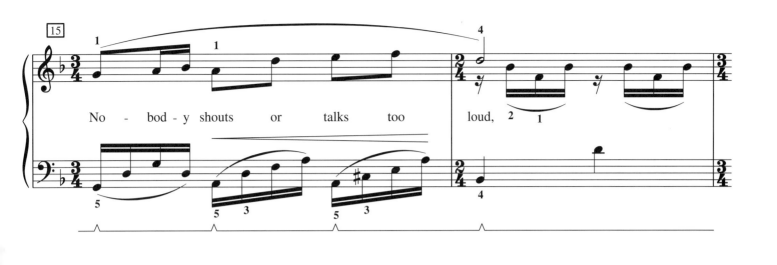

No - bod - y shouts or talks too loud,

not in my cas - tle on a cloud.

There is a la - dy all in white, _ holds me and sings a lul - la - by. She's

nice to see and she's soft to touch. She says, "Co-sette, I love you ver - y much."

I know a place where no one's lost.

I know a place where no one cries.

Cry - ing at all is not al - lowed, not in my cas - tle on a

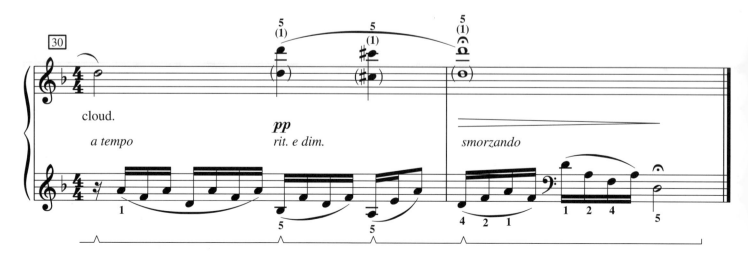

cloud.